Kitchens

COUNTRY LIVING

EASY TRANSFORMATIONS

Kitchens

Cynthia D'Aprix Sweeney

HEARST BOOKS

A division of Sterling Publishing Co., Inc.

New York / London
www.sterlingpublishing.com

A Primrose Productions Book
Designed by Stephanie Stislow

Photography Credits: Front Jacket and Spine: Keith Scott Morton; Back Jacket: upper left: Natasha Milne; upper right: William P. Steele; bottom left: Keith Scott Morton

Library of Congress Cataloging-in-Publication Data on file.

10 9 8 7 6 5 4 3 2 1

First Paperback Edition 2008
Published by Hearst Books
A Division of Sterling Publishing Co., Inc.
387 Park Avenue South, New York, NY 10016

Country Living and Hearst Books are trademarks of Hearst Communications, Inc.

www.countryliving.com

For information about custom editions, special sales, premium and corporate purchases, please contact Sterling Special Sales Department at 800-805-5489 or specialsales@sterlingpub.com.

Distributed in Canada by Sterling Publishing
C/o Canadian Manda Group, 165 Dufferin Street
Toronto, Ontario, Canada M6K 3H6

Distributed in Australia by Capricorn Link (Australia) Pty. Ltd.
P.O. Box 704, Windsor, NSW 2756 Australia

Manufactured in China

Sterling ISBN 13: 978-1-58816-577-0
        ISBN 10: 1-58816-577-9

Contents

Foreword

As a veteran of two kitchen remodels, I can attest to the challenges involved in such an undertaking. There are so many questions regarding color schemes, cabinetry, flooring, appliances, seating, and storage. It can be daunting, to say the least. But few projects are as important to the harmony of our homes, since so many of our treasured memories with family and friends are made from moments that take place in this room.

Kitchens simplifies the process of renovating. Are you struggling to squeeze many amenities into a small space? Tempted to work with bold, bright colors? Wondering how to incorporate collections into a decorating scheme? We'll show you how. On the pages ahead, you'll see more than 100 beautiful, welcoming kitchens and learn how you can transfer the looks into your own home. Whether you're planning an overhaul or merely looking for a few ways to spruce up what you have, this book will give you the confidence to make it happen.

NANCY MERNIT SORIANO

Editor-in-Chief

Country Living

L E F T : This kitchen is a sublime mix of old and new. The generously proportioned farmhouse double sink anchors the room. Original cabinetry comes to life with a fresh coat of paint and period-style hardware. The painted gray floor and poured concrete countertop gently nudge the room into the present.

Introduction

The kitchen is the heart of the home—the place we go to celebrate, nourish, console, and reflect. Our connection to the kitchen is both genuinely emotional and—by necessity—extremely practical. It's no wonder that most home renovations begin with the kitchen. No other room in the house needs to be so many different things: an efficient workspace, a gathering spot for family and friends, and a gracious expression of a home's style.

Over the past few decades, the kitchen has grown, both literally and figuratively, in our lives. In the early 1970s, the average North American kitchen was 150 square feet (about 14 square meters), which was, typically, approximately 9% of a home's overall space. Today, the average kitchen has doubled in size, representing almost 12% of the house. As our lifestyles have become more hectic and demanding, our definition of the ideal kitchen has also evolved. *Kitchens* recognizes the challenges inherent in creating a room that's both beautiful and useful.

When considering an overall look for your kitchen, the usual starting point is the era in which your home was built or the period its current style reflects. But a kitchen's look doesn't have to conform to rigid historical or style definitions. In fact, designing or updating a kitchen is also an excellent opportunity to push the design envelope a bit and mix things up. As you'll see in the following pages, today's country kitchen comes in many different shapes, styles, and colors. In the kitchens you'll see in this book, modern appliances blend seamlessly with family heirlooms; industrial chic provides the perfect backdrop for a collection of vintage pottery. It's never been easier to find new cabinets that play as antique, or to mix flea-market treasures with contemporary finishes. Found objects—a garden gate, an old dresser, a dramatic piece of molding—can take on new life in a variety of useful and decorative ways.

In many homes, the kitchen has replaced the formal dining room as the primary place to break bread. As you reconsider your kitchen's style, think carefully about what you'll require from the room. The utility of a kitchen remains a critical factor in most design decisions. The all-important work triangle (efficient distance between sink, fridge, and stove) must anchor your room's layout. It's equally important to analyze the way you cook and entertain as you choose and position furnishings. Your kitchen should possess distinct areas for working and seating, but should also be adaptable to different situations.

Perhaps the biggest challenge in any kitchen is efficient—and attractive—storage. Almost every chapter in this book offers creative storage solutions, from new and inventive ideas for built-ins to simple, quick suggestions, like a pretty basket brimming with linens. You can find a multitude of ways to maximize your storage while retaining—and even highlighting—the country look and feel of your room.

Whether your kitchen is on a quiet, meandering country road or high above the city streets, *Kitchens* will help you transform your space into an authentic reflection of your personal style and history. From small inspirations to big ideas, this book offers food for thought and is the first step to creating the kitchen of your dreams.

Finding the Right Style

Whether you're facing a complete redesign or just looking to give your existing space a facelift, there are many places to look for inspiration. Though you may start out feeling overwhelmed by all the possibilities, few of us begin with a truly blank slate when choosing a particular style for our kitchen. Start by thinking about the era of your home. If you're in a Victorian townhouse or a turn-of-the-century cabin, your design parameters are easy to identify. If you're working with new construction, however, your options are much wider.

What looks do you admire in other rooms? What kinds of objects do you love? Which of your existing possessions–a teapot collection, an heirloom table, a treasured vintage stove–might inspire you to create the kitchen of your dreams? Maybe you'd like a space that reminds you of the comforts of your grandmother's kitchen. Or perhaps you imagine yourself cooking in a kitchen with a clean, modern feel.

Keep in mind that "country" is all about making your space personal and warm. Whether your choices are vintage or modern, they will help shape your interpretation of country style. There are a multitude of looks that say, "Come in. Welcome to my kitchen. Relax and be nourished."

LEFT: The Shaker style is particularly appropriate for kitchens since its beauty derives from attention to detail and an austere simplicity. The cabinet pulls, highly polished wood countertop, and clean white cabinets give this room a classic Shaker look. Navy woven cord seats add depth to the room.

RIGHT: This classic country kitchen houses an impressive collection of antique furniture and objects yet still functions as an efficient workspace. The use of muted, period colors on the cabinetry, walls, and molding sets the scene, while details such as the cast-iron pot hanging from the ceiling reinforce the early American theme. An old armoire, a hanging yellow cupboard, and traditional soapstone countertops impart authentic farmhouse ambience.

USING AN ANTIQUE TABLE TO BACK UP THE ISLAND GIVES THE ROOM ANOTHER VINTAGE DECORATIVE DETAIL AND AN ADDITIONAL WORK SURFACE.

LEFT: The timeless all-white palette is a popular choice for kitchens. White lends a clean and calm feel to a room that's often bustling with activity. This kitchen's all-white look is subtly accented with contrasting black counters and hardware. The window-pane design on the higher cabinetry provides an Arts and Crafts touch.

CAREFUL ATTENTION HAS BEEN PAID TO DETAILS IN THIS KITCHEN; IN PARTICULAR, THE MOLDING AND TRIM, WHICH LEND A SUBTLE VINTAGE FEELING.

A GLASS SHELF TOPPED WITH DELICATE TRANSPARENT OBJECTS DRESSES UP THIS WINDOW WITHOUT BLOCKING THE LIGHT OR VIEW.

A B O V E : Want to modernize a traditional room? Take some tips from this quick-yet-effective transformation: Shaker-style cabinets take on a modern attitude when painted a cool color. A honed granite countertop, stainless appliances, and a striped throw rug easily update a traditional kitchen.

L E F T : A city kitchen high in the sky can still reflect the country spirit. The glass-front and recessed-panel cabinet doors, paired with rich crown molding, give this room a country feel. Extending the countertop beneath the window and above a radiator creates instant counter space—with a view.

THE CALL OF THE WILD:
MULE DEER ANTLERS
MAKE STRIKING DRAWER
AND CABINET PULLS.

LOOK TO YOUR ENVIRONMENT
FOR INSPIRATION. SMALL PIECES
OF BARBED WIRE ELEVATE THESE
PENDANT LIGHTS FROM ORDINARY
TO REMARKABLE.

L E F T: Rustic takes on a whole new dimension in this
beautifully designed log-cabin kitchen. When working
with a dark-hued room, paint surfaces in pale tones—
an ideal way to lighten the scene. Here, soft blue
cabinets stand out against the home's unfinished
interior walls. Intricate "twig" custom cabinetry provides
a dramatic impact.

Steal This Idea

Hang a functional object in an unexpected spot. This vintage clock breaks the surface of the beaded-board backsplash and is perfectly placed to help a cook to keep track of time.

Other useful items to hang in an otherwise unused spot:

• a blackboard or corkboard

• a kitchen towel rod or hook

• spice racks

• a radio or CD player

• a knife rack

EMBOSSED MOLDING GIVES
AN OLD-WORLD LOOK TO
THE METALLIC WALL TILES
SURROUNDING THE RANGE.

ABOVE: Modern, industrial finishes can still take on country appeal, as demonstrated by this gleaming kitchen. The oak farmhouse table and colorful wood chairs provide a warm contrast to the austere stainless cabinetry.

ABOVE: This kitchen shows how cool, contemporary architecture can be complemented by a warm, country feel. Open shelving displays rustic baskets, colorful linens, favorite books, and treasured collectibles—creating a casual and personal feeling. The light-toned wood softens the stainless-steel countertops.

ABOVE: Decorative themes that might be overpowering in another room can be ideal in a kitchen, particularly if you're an avid collector of a certain period. Entering this room feels like taking a step back in time. The checkered linoleum floor and vintage table and chairs all work perfectly with antique linens and collectibles. Not for the faint of heart, this room is a love letter to a particular era.

SIMPLE, UNEMBELLISEHED CABINETRY IS A GOOD BACK-DROP FOR AN EXUBERANT COLLECTION.

RIGHT: Where better than the kitchen to display your sense of fun and whimsy? Flea-market finds provided inspiration for this room's look. The colorful walls and molding reflect the mix-and-match pottery collection. A vintage sign provides an interesting focal point.

It's Easy Being Green

Most of the waste we generate originates in the kitchen, so it makes sense to put some thought into designing an earth-friendly room.

- Include easily accessible recycling containers in your design; you'll be more likely to be conscientious about your recycling responsibilities.
- Consider bamboo as an alternative to other woods. Serene, strong, and sustainable, bamboo makes for striking floors, countertops, and even backsplashes.
- Make sure your appliances are energy efficient. Convection ovens use less energy than conventional ovens. And top-bottom refrigerator-freezers are more efficient than the side-by-side models.
- Install low-voltage or fluorescent lighting.

Steal This Idea

Not ready to commit to a vintage appliance? Skittish about a strong color scheme? The answer is to start small.

- Flea markets and antique shops are good sources for smaller vintage appliances such as toasters or can openers that you can pick up inexpensively and display in almost any style kitchen. If you find the look appealing, you can move on up to larger vintage pieces such as stoves and refrigerators.

- Vintage accessories such as salt-and-pepper shakers and napkin dispensers are also in plentiful supply, and represent a good opportunity to experiment with period color and style in your kitchen.

If you decide that just a few spots of color or a few hints of the past are enough, your collectibles will add personality to your space. If you're even more enthused about the period items, you'll have the confidence to make a bolder change.

RIGHT: Vintage pink appliances turn this basic white kitchen into a retro showcase. An old-fashioned linoleum floor and diner-style table and chairs complete the look.

A Gathering Place

A kitchen has two equally important roles in any home. It is a room for work, of course, and needs to be practical and efficient. But the kitchen is also a social room—very much the heart of your home—the place where family and friends gather to eat and reconnect. To ensure that your new or redesigned kitchen fulfills both roles well, before you begin your work, think hard about your kitchen space, your needs as a cook, and how you like to entertain.

Are you the type of cook who prefers to work alone? If so, you'll need plenty of elbow room, and you'll want your guests seated away from the action. Do you like to hand over a vegetable peeler or cutting board and involve your friends or children in food prep? In that case, a nice spacious center island with plenty of seating should figure into your design.

Do you host enormous feasts for the neighborhood or is a small, intimate dinner more your style? Most of us need the flexibility to occasionally do both. You may need lots of in-kitchen seating or a separate dining area. Providing the right spaces for people to congregate takes a small amount of foresight and planning, but reaps huge benefits.

DON'T LET A GENEROUSLY PROPORTIONED WINDOWSILL GO UNDRESSED. A PIECE OF POTTERY, A SET OF FRAMED PHOTOS, OR A SMALL BOUQUET CAN ADD VISUAL INTEREST TO ANY ROOM.

LEFT: Many rooms have an unused corner that can be transformed into a cozy breakfast nook, eliminating the need for a large table in the center of your kitchen. This corner housed two windows, so a small amount of light was sacrificed for this elegant nook. The striped, colorful upholstery is decorative and stain-resistant. The wicker table adds a touch of fun.

LEFT: This island countertop extends beyond the cabinetry to provide a welcoming perch for friends and family. The expansive, stylish breakfast nook offers more formal seating for any time of day.

BROWN AND WHITE TRANSFERWARE PLATES ARE A NICE DECORATIVE TOUCH AND ALSO PROVIDE PALETTE INSPIRATION FOR UPHOLSTERED PILLOWS.

CounterPoints

- Consider blending different types of countertops in your home for maximum efficiency. Wood is best for chopping and slicing. Marble is the first choice for bakers. And stone or tile resists heat.
- If you have the space for a pastry area, drop the countertop by a few inches for easier rolling and kneading.
- If building from scratch, choose the right countertop height for the various members of your family who will be working in the kitchen. But keep in mind that anything that deviates too far from standard measurements could impact the resale value of your home.

R I G H T : This extra-long counter neatly bisects the kitchen from the living area. Using an open counter in place of a wall joins the two spaces together and creates a warm and inviting room for working, dining, and entertaining. The generously proportioned counter allows for cut-out seating and still provides plenty of cabinet space on either side.

WHEN THE COOKING YIELDS TO ENTERTAINING, A PAIR OF LAMPS OFFERS A SOFTER GLOW THAN THE BRIGHT TASK LIGHTING NEEDED FOR FOOD PREP.

BENCHES ARE A SMART SEATING SOLUTION. THEY CAN BE USED DECORATIVELY IN A VARIETY OF PLACES AND PRESSED INTO SERVICE WHEN EXTRA SPACE IS NEEDED. AN UNEXPECTED GUEST? EVERYONE JUST SITS A LITTLE CLOSER!

ABOVE: This weathered farmhouse table is a pleasant surprise in a kitchen that features a contemporary look. The sleek modern chairs are a nice juxtaposition with the table's lovely aged patina.

LEFT: An antique farmhouse table works in almost any setting. Whether the table is an original or a reproduction, its distressed surface adds texture and a sense of history to any room.

ABOVE: The raised back on this island creates a nice ledge for entertaining. It works as well for a casual family moment (winter afternoon hot cocoa) as it does for a more formal event (a cocktail bar during a party). The back of the island also serves as a visual shield from the inevitable clutter of cooking. This feature is particularly valuable in houses without separate dining rooms.

A B O V E : Armchairs are an unexpected but welcome addition to any kitchen. This seating area is a great spot to curl up with a good book and a cup of tea while keeping an eye on what's in the oven. Slipcovers make it easy to change looks or launder stains from occasional spills.

RIGHT: This center island offers two different heights and surfaces, creating a truly useful workstation. The elevated half, with a traditional soapstone surface, houses a second sink, perfect for an extra pair of hands. The lower half of the island is covered with more durable butcher block and is the right height for chopping and baking.

IF YOU ENJOY COOKING WITH COMPANY, ARRANGE YOUR KITCHEN SO THAT THE "WORK TRIANGLES" (FOR EXAMPLE, SINK-REFRIGERATOR-COUNTERTOP AND OVEN-COUNTERTOP-SINK) DO NOT OVERLAP. THAT WILL ALLOW TWO (OR MORE) COOKS TO WORK SMOOTHLY ALONGSIDE ONE ANOTHER WITHOUT INTERFERING WITH EACH OTHER'S MOVEMENTS.

Open and Airy

Enhancing the interplay between space and light is a key to successful kitchen design. A well-designed room offers visual equilibrium: the right mix of light and dark, uplifting illumination along with a sense of being grounded.

If you're lucky enough to have a double-height room, cathedral ceilings, or floor-to-ceiling windows, much of the work has been done for you. Abundant natural light and a spacious layout also make for great raw material. But you still need a smart design eye to pull the elements together and show the room's natural gifts off to their best advantage.

Even a small, windowless kitchen can be made to exude an open and airy attitude. Maximizing the natural light you do have, adding multiple sources and layers of light, and using color and texture to lighten and reflect—these and other ideas can help transform a formerly poky kitchen into a room that blooms.

LIGHT FIXTURES PLACED NEAR THE CEILING CONTINUE TO ILLUMINATE THE SPACE WHEN THE SUN GOES DOWN.

LEFT: It's not just the striking vaulted ceiling that gives this room its impact. The four windows set high above the room let in abundant natural light and provide a dramatic focal point. The slate backsplash (which echoes the window design above) draws the eye downward and matches the slate floor and countertop below. Maple woodwork lightly balances the room.

RIGHT: While this room enjoys a barrel-vaulted ceiling, other simple touches—such as the minimal use of hanging cabinetry, plus the tranparent glass in their doors—enhance its roomy feel. Open space above the cabinets highlights the high ceilings. The slim, tapered legs of the Shaker table and chairs blend nicely with the wooden floors and contribute to the spacious feel of this room.

REFLECTIVE SURFACES SUBTLY INCREASE THE AMOUNT OF LIGHT IN THE ROOM.

ABOVE: A small kitchen with low ceilings presents the biggest challenge for manufacturing light and space. Here, a cutout over the sink lets additional light and air into the room.

DOUBLE SINKS ARE COMMON IN KITCHENS, BUT HOW ABOUT TWO SETS OF FAUCETS? IT'S AN INSPIRED IDEA THAT ALLOWS TWO PEOPLE TO WORK AT ONCE.

LEFT: Eliminating cabinets above the countertop in favor of open shelving gives this narrow kitchen a bigger and brighter feel. Light floods in via the added breakfast nook, illuminating the room's original wide-plank floors. The display shelves near the ceiling draw the eye up toward the pretty beaded-board ceiling.

RIGHT : This room doesn't have particularly high ceilings, but a few simple tricks make it seem open and bright. A painted white floor opens the entire space. Colorful striped rugs protect heavily trafficked areas and add a splash of style. The glass tile backsplash is reminiscent of beach glass, perfect for this waterside retreat.

RECTANGULAR CABINETS
ELONGATE THE SPACE.

LEFT: This relatively small space shows how the proper balance of light and dark can make all the difference in a tight space. The rich, gleaming wood floor and counter-top could overwhelm the room, but with walls, molding and ceiling all painted white, the final effect is one of light, grounded by wood. Similarly, the white beaded-board and cabinetry temper the dark wood of the island.

ABOVE: The popular center island can interrupt the visual flow of a room. Leaving the bottom of the island open creates a visual lightness. Use the space to display objects of similar shapes and sizes. Keep it neat and decorative. The surface of this island, which is poured concrete, was stained a delicate blue to further lighten the room.

Tips for Small Kitchens

- Reduce clutter by increasing built-ins. Built-ins may be costly, but they are well worth it: reducing clutter is a key element to making a small room seem larger.

- Use every inch. Often, there are small spaces in kitchens that aren't big enough for a cabinet but can easily be turned into a narrow storage space. If you have such a space, consider turning it into a slide-out pantry (pictured) or a spot to store cookie sheets or cookbooks.

- Edit your gadgets. Do you really need an espresso machine, an electric mixer, a bean grinder, a juicer, a food processor, an electric knife sharpener… you get the idea. Donate things you don't use on a regular basis. And store the "occasional" items out of sight, in the basement or in those hard-to-reach cabinets near the ceiling.

- Look up. Hang pots and pans from a ceiling rack. Install shelves up near the ceiling to display attractive ceramics or pottery.

RIGHT: Nothing expands a room like bringing the outdoors in. Take advantage of a bank of windows or French doors by placing your table directly in front. A room with a view gives the illusion that the room extends beyond its natural borders.

Turn Up the Heat
with Color

Color is a terrific way to add character and personality to your kitchen. You can add color in a big way—a bright coat of paint; in select areas—a bold area rug; or in spots—a collection of Fiestaware®. Any of these can lift a room from ordinary to extraordinary. Remember, too, that color need not be flat; introducing contrast with paint, fabric, or finishes is another way to bring color into your kitchen.

When choosing color, consider how different shades affect your mood. If you have to make it through a cold, dark winter, a coat of bright yellow paint on your cabinets might be just the tonic. If your rooms are always flooded with sun, cobalt blue will have a deep, dramatic effect. The important thing is not to be intimidated by color.

Inspiration for your kitchen palette is all around you. Does the Japanese maple in the backyard lift your spirits? Why not bring that color into the room with pottery or fabric? That platter from Tuscany sitting in your kitchen cabinet can be the perfect starting point for the right shade of green. Start small, build confidence with some touches of color, and then work up to that fire-engine red ceiling you've been dreaming of.

LEFT: The canvas of this kitchen is pure white with the exception of the vintage stove. Color is carefully applied through furniture and vibrant collectibles. The red-and-white canister collection is flamboyant but not overpowering.

RIGHT: Embracing a decidedly Southwestern look, this kitchen demonstrates the value of strong colors in even a small room. The deep blue cabinets, terra-cotta tiles, and yellow walls are bold and inviting. The colorful back-splash tiles work as a unifying touch.

IF YOU'RE WORRIED A COLOR MIGHT FEEL TOO STRONG ON CABINETS, CONSIDER LETTING THE CENTER OF EACH DOOR REMAIN NEUTRAL. HERE, PRESSED TIN SOFTENS THE DEEP BLUE. OTHER OPTIONS ARE GLASS OR A LIGHTER, CONTRASTING SHADE.

ABOVE: Choosing a strong secondary color is a surefire way to liven up your kitchen. Red provides a vivid contrast to the soft white and celery-green shades in this room. Enormous red crepe-paper flowers add an unexpected flair.

LEFT: Saffron walls, teal cabinets, bright pottery, and Mexican fabrics come together in a joyful explosion of color. The vibrant vintage pottery collection acts as both inspiration and focal point in this room.

Color Sense

- Paint chips are helpful for narrowing your choices, but you need to see the color on your wall to truly decide if it works. Paint a large (3 feet x 3 feet or 90 cm x 90 cm) test square in your room. Examine the color in all lights. A shade you love in the early morning sun might be unbearable at night under artificial light.

- Choosing the "wrong" white can be catastrophic in a room. Every shade of white will have an undertone: pink, yellow, blue, and so on. Use paint chips to compare the undertone of the white you choose with your secondary colors.

- Wood counts as color, too. Make sure the colors you're testing blend nicely with the wood tones in the room.

- You can always go custom. If you're having a hard time finding the color you want, you can bring a piece of fabric or a tile sample into the hardware store and have the clerk mix a custom color for you. If you do this, be sure you order enough paint. Different batches of color can have a very different look.

LEFT: This room exemplifies bold restraint. The deep blue floor and walls could have made this room feel claustrophobic. But the bright white ceiling and trim soften the effect. The oversized pale-blue vintage sink brings the whole look together. Because the touches of red have the same tonal quality as the deep blue, they work nicely together.

RIGHT: Intentionally busy, this kitchen celebrates its flea-market heritage with color abundant. No surface is ignored. Sponge-painting on the cabinets, gingham tie-back curtains, vintage decals, and farm signs add up to a down-home look.

MIX AND MATCH VINTAGE CHAIRS. WHENEVER YOU SEE ONE YOU LIKE, PICK IT UP. THEY CAN BE DISTRIBUTED THROUGH YOUR HOME OR PLACED TOGETHER AROUND A TABLE FOR AN ECLECTIC LOOK.

Cool Comfort

For all its heat, the kitchen is also the place we turn to for cool refreshment. It's no wonder that white is such a popular choice for kitchens. White is crisp, clean, and calm—all excellent qualities for a room in which we prepare and enjoy meals.

The key to designing a clean kitchen that also feels warm and inviting is to avoid a clinical, operating-room feeling. If you're starting with a white canvas for your kitchen, think about also adding complementary hues, interesting textures, natural touches, and accessories that reflect your personality or the ambience you want your kitchen to project.

If you want to maintain the all-white palette, you might add texture with stone, tile, or fabric. If your kitchen boasts a pleasing view, let it become a focal point. Collectibles, flea-market finds, and unique accessories all stand out with white as their backdrop.

Consider finally, whether it is actually white that you want, or a cool palette that features a soft, light hue. A cool blue or soft green used for cabinets or countertops will enhance the serenity of your space and help you to achieve that feeling of cool comfort but with a hint of color.

L E F T : The absence of color and clever use of stainless steel are the defining characteristics of this room. Open cubes display grouped glassware in a way that's almost curatorial, but not the least bit stuffy. A strong eye for balance and symmetry give this room its style.

LEFT: The ubiquitous center island is another great place to introduce color. Here, a soft blue adds panache to an ivory room. Glass doors on the island cabinetry provide a peek at cake stands, glassware, and books—and add depth to the workspace.

BASKETRY IS A STAPLE OF COUNTRY LIVING. LOOK FOR INTERESTING EXAMPLES, LIKE THIS HANDCRAFTED HAMPER WITH WOODEN HANDLES.

Buying a Vintage Appliance

- Consider choosing a contemporary replica of an antique appliance. You won't have to worry about costly repairs or refurbishing.
- If authenticity is your focus, be prepared to sacrifice a few modern conveniences like ice makers and automatic oven cleaning. The upside? You'll save energy without all the bells and whistles common on contemporary appliances.
- If you're considering an old or old-looking appliance, move it to the top of your to-do list. A beautiful antique stove or bright vintage refrigerator can be the key design element in your space.

ABOVE: If you're ready for a long-term commitment, consider a vintage appliance (or two) for your kitchen. Whether they're purely decorative (like an old gas range used for display) or meant to be functional like the refrigerator pictured, they're a wonderful design component and a great conversation piece.

RIGHT: If you find a color you love, think about making it your primary shade. White becomes the accent color in this tranquil robin's-egg blue room. Even the lavastone countertop is a perfect match for the soothing color of the cabinets, unifying the room in an unusually strong way. White glazed pottery echoes the subway tile backsplash.

DON'T BE AFRAID TO MIX ARCHITECTURAL DETAILS EVEN IN A SMALL GALLEY KITCHEN. THESE CABINETS HAVE THREE DIFFERENT STYLES OF DOOR FRONTS—BEADED BOARD, SOLID, AND GLASS—AND ARE PAIRED WITH OVERSIZED DENTIL MOLDING. THE EFFECT IS SPECTACULAR.

ABOVE: With light flooding in from above and a windowed wall open to the backyard, this kitchen is all about inviting nature indoors. The soft palette and stone floor offer a soothing backdrop to the view.

TWO SIDE-BY-SIDE SINKS ARE SET AT DIFFERENT HEIGHTS FOR DIFFERENT TASKS. ONE IS HIGH, PERFECT FOR WASHING VEGETABLES AND FRUITS; THE OTHER IS SET LOWER WITH A GOOSENECK FAUCET THAT IS JUST RIGHT FOR SCRUBBING POTS.

LEFT: Two-toned cabinets offer a nice balance of white and green and highlight the elegance of the Shaker-inspired design.

RIGHT: Blue and white is a classic combination for any room in your house. In this kitchen, a bluestone countertop and sink add a splash of color that gives the room an authentic period look. A combination of open and closed storage allows collectibles to be displayed but prevents any feeling of clutter. The plate racks, painted to match the counter, display English ceramic ware.

AN AREA RUG IN THE KITCHEN IS A GREAT WAY TO EFFECT A QUICK CHANGE—AND IT IS EASY TO ADD (OR SUBTRACT) ACCORDING TO YOUR MOOD.

Pattern Play

Introducing pattern to a kitchen is a sophisticated way to add visual depth and interest. Patterns occur naturally in kitchens—in the panes of a window, in wide-planked floors, in the grout lines between tiles. You can exaggerate an existing pattern or add entirely new textures and shapes through patterned fabric, paint, or accessories.

Patterns will work best in a room if you follow a few simple tenets. When mixing patterns, keep the colors complementary. Remember that matching tones will unite the different elements of your space in a pleasing way. If you're looking for bold touches, keep them small. A gingham curtain or seat cushion, for example, adds a country touch but is not overwhelming.

Keep in mind that whether your kitchen is cool and elegant, casual farmhouse or flea market chic, a touch of whimsy is never out of place.

USING AN EXTRA-WIDE GROUT LINE IN A CONTRASTING COLOR HAS A DRAMATIC EFFECT. KEEP IN MIND THAT TILE ISN'T A PARTICULARLY DURABLE COUNTERTOP SURFACE. IF YOU'RE WORRIED ABOUT HAVING TO REGROUT A COUNTER, USE THIS IDEA ON A BACKSPLASH OR FLOOR INSTEAD.

LEFT: This kitchen makes creative use of a variety of patterns, beginning with the blue-and-white tiles on the range backsplash. A striped rug and under-sink curtains in matching colors finish the look.

ABOVE: This room's geometric patterns—the black-and-white diamond floor and the square windowpanes on the French doors—find echoes in the black-and-white palette of the kitchen, the glass-front cabinets, and the neatly arranged glassware above the cabinetry. The attention to balance and symmetry give this room its sophisticated charm.

A B O V E : Colorful red and yellow squares mix masterfully with the neutral and wood tones. This bold pattern contributes a colorful flair to the sleekly modern look of the rest of the kitchen.

Create A Checkerboard Floor

- Start with a clean (freshly sanded, if necessary) floor.
- Choose a square size appropriate for the room's scale.
- Using a pencil and ruler, lightly trace outlines of the pattern on floor.
- Outline dark squares with blue painter's tape to prevent dark color from seeping into the lighter squares.
- Apply dark paint with a brush, consistently pulling the brush inward from the tape.
- Remove tape and wipe off any excess stain or paint with a cloth.
- When dry, seal with polyurethane.

ABOVE: Forget what your mother told you about mixing stripes and checks. Done the right way, the impact is dramatic and fitting. The black-and-white color scheme unifies contrasting looks in an elegant way. Upholstered chairs are a gracious touch in even the most casual setting.

LEFT: Like to add a pattern to your room but can't decide where? Look down. A simple wooden floor is a perfect place for the extra panache provided by pattern. The black diamond on this floor is elegant and creates a visual bridge into the next room.

L E F T : The beaded-board lines on the cabinetry and horizontal open shelves are a nice contrast to the black-and-white check walls. This effect was created by using small white tiles and a contrasting grout.

CREATE PATTERNS BY GROUPING IDENTICAL ITEMS ON OPEN SHELVES—A PRACTICAL AND ATTRACTIVE SOLUTION.

A TILED FLOOR IS AN OPPORTUNITY TO CREATE PATTERNS—AND TO DIFFERENTIATE AREAS WITHIN THE SPACE BY VARYING THE PATTERN.

A B O V E : A sunny palette allows a variety of patterns to work together in this cheerful kitchen. Buttery walls form a warm background. The terra-cotta tiles are set in diagonal and rectangular patterns, picking up on the panes in the doors and the under-counter wine rack. Prints grace the upholstery and the lampshades, while a sunflower motif makes the table a whimsically unique focal point.

Steal this Idea

Use fabric in place of cabinet
doors—a colorful and inexpensive
way to give your cabinetry a facelift.

Display as Design

One of the qualities that makes a kitchen special is that it's brimming with life. Unfortunately, that also usually means it's brimming with stuff. The difference between a kitchen filled with clutter and one that artfully displays objects is organization and technique.

First, take stock of your stuff. Some kitchen accoutrements are naturally elegant or attractive—an Italian espresso machine, a fancy toaster, the iconic countertop mixer. Everyday objects can be decorative, too. Decide what you want to keep visible and easily accessible; store the rest behind closed cabinet doors, in drawers, or even in another room.

The trick to display as design is to reveal the inner workings of a kitchen in a way that is visually symmetrical and logical—by color, shape, or texture. Artfully arranged glassware, colorful plates on a shelf, and even supplies such as bottled water or laundry detergent can be ornamental if displayed properly.

LEFT: The choice of clear glass panels fronting pots and pans is unusual but really works in this kitchen. The glass eliminates the need to open and close cabinet doors to find what you're looking for. And being able to see the interior of the cabinet adds a nice depth to the space. The long stainless handles mimic the rectangular shapes of the glass panes and the stainless countertop above.

L E F T : Open shelving and storage are key to a display-as-design look. This eclectic kitchen incorporates several different options, including a wall-mounted hanging rack, open space below the island, and bracket-supported wall shelves.

A B O V E : This colorful display successfully mixes and matches different types of ceramics because the colors are complementary. When blending or building a collection of differing objects, pay attention to color and tone.

SCAN YOUR KITCHEN WITH AN EYE TO
UNUSED SPACE THAT MIGHT BE IDEAL
FOR HANGING DISPLAY SHELVES—LIKE
THE SPACE BETWEEN TWO WINDOWS.

ABOVE: Enamel is the unifying element in this collection. The pitchers and pots—even the 1930s range—all work together because of their similar surface. Vintage appliances might not be practical or desirable as functioning pieces in every kitchen, but used as a showcase, they're both useful and beautiful.

SPACE BENEATH YOUR FURNITURE CAN ALSO BE USED FOR DISPLAY, AS THESE PITCHERS SHOW, TUCKED OUT OF THE WAY BUT STILL IN PLAIN SIGHT.

ABOVE: Think out of the kitchen box. Displaying an antique toy boat collection plays on the location of this lakefront home and adds a refreshing, non-culinary touch to the room.

Steal This Idea

Make art from storage. Here, each item is a perfect fit for the height of the shelves. "White space" is minimized and the colors red and green are repeated throughout.

THE AREA ABOVE AN APPLIANCE IS USUALLY LEFT BARE, BUT THAT SPACE CAN BE USEFUL. IN THIS ROOM, THE HANGING VINTAGE CHAIR FILLS THAT SPACE AND BECOMES THE FOCAL POINT, REFRAMING AN ORDINARY APPLIANCE.

RIGHT: Take a page from the Pop-Art movement and discover the beauty in your groceries. These open shelves make the most of the lively graphics and colors of ordinary household items. The key to executing this look successfully is to use recurring colors and the right shapes.

LEFT: Collections don't have to be uniform to work together. The open shelving and island in this kitchen display a mishmash of objects without looking messy. One reason is the repeated use of red, white, and blue. In addition, small groupings of similar objects reduce the visual cacophony.

BUY DISH TOWELS IN BRIGHT COLORS AND KEEP THEM ON DISPLAY. HANDY TO GRAB FOR THE OCCASIONAL SPILL, THEY ALSO ADD TEXTURE TO THE ROOM.

RIGHT: A monochromatic look is a neat way to unify a mix of pieces. This collection encompasses different styles and types of objects, but because everything is white, it all goes together. Transparent glass is a smart way to round out your collectibles because it mixes with any color. Painting the shelves white and setting them against a colored background makes the collection pop.

Care of Vintage Linens

- When shopping for vintage linens, check carefully for stains and only buy a discolored item if you can live with its condition. Any stain you take home with you is most likely there to stay.
- If you want to keep the antique linens you own in perfect condition, use them "gently"—for display or on a table that won't be used for dining.
- Buy cloths or curtains in different colors and themes. They can easily be switched according to seasons or holidays, giving your kitchen a fresh look.
- Fine pieces should be washed by hand. Never use bleach, which will gradually break down the fibers of aged cloth. If you have a persistent stain, try removing it with diluted lemon juice.

ABOVE: This eye-catching plate rack provides easy access to a high-use item. The rack also protects fragile plates from chips and cracks that can occur more frequently when plates are stacked.

THE INEXPENSIVE OPEN SHELVING GIVES AN AIRY LOOK TO THE ENTIRE INSTALLATION.

LEFT: These stainless shelves, outfitted with sleek steel baskets, came from a restaurant supply house. The baskets offer ample storage for linens and cutlery.

ABOVE: Collections need not be large to have impact. Small groupings of similar shapes and colors set on open shelving give this simple kitchen a distinctive personality.

RIGHT: Don't overlook the structure of your shelving. The Arts and Crafts design of this side bracket adds extra visual interest to the display.

Past and Present

An artful blend of past and present is a key component to successful country kitchen design. The kitchens here approach the challenge creatively, whether introducing vintage elements to a new space or situating modern pieces in traditional environments.

A simple and fun way to give a modern space classic character is to collect things (not necessarily with kitchen or food-related themes) that make you reminisce, spark an emotional connection, or simply delight your eye. Then focus on artfully displaying your found objects. You don't need to have amassed a huge collection before you show your treasures—even one or two intriguing items from days gone by can impart a sense of another era to your kitchen. Old-style architectural elements and antique furniture are equally transformative.

By virtue of their simplicity of their clean lines, modern pieces often integrate easily and beautifully into old-fashioned rooms. The crucial ingredient in this recipe of old and new is confidence, as the kitchens in this chapter show.

LEFT: If you love old furniture but want to give it a cleaner look, a fresh coat of paint and new hardware will do the trick. This 1930s Hoosier cabinet, used to display a pewter collection, gets a whimsical touch with two different types of hardware.

Steal This Idea

Creative adaptation of old finds to new uses is a hallmark of the country kitchen. This room has numerous examples:

• Reclaimed banister spindles divide cookie sheets and baking pans

• An old garden gate becomes a pot rack— and old washtubs and ewers find display space on top

• A rustic table holds a microwave oven

RIGHT: This kitchen says "country" in a variety of subtle ways. The painted farmhouse table, surrounded by an assortment of flea-market stools, serves as a bright and cheery center island. White brings it all together.

INSTEAD OF INSTALLING CABINETRY, GIVE AN OLD SIDEBOARD A FRESH COAT OF PAINT AND FIT IT WITH A SINK.

A B O V E : Found objects placed together make an interesting installation. A salvaged pillar takes on new heights when topped with a rusted white colander.

L E F T : Introduce the unexpected! An old country headboard—inverted and hung above the range-hood mantel—functions as an inventive fleur-de-lis for this French country room.

A B O V E : An old apothecary chest surrounded by a collection of antique mortars and pestles imparts an old-world beauty to this room.

R I G H T : The centerpiece of this kitchen is an antique butcher-block table that's been fitted with wheels and a steel meat rack on top. Wheels on the island make it a moveable piece when entertaining large groups. The meat rack transforms into an extravagant pot rack.

LEFT: A collection of vintage kitchenware finds a home in this space, in which a salvaged sign hanging in the pass-through says it all. Unobtrusive in plain white, modern appliances don't detract from the room's old-fashioned ambience.

AN OLD TABLE ADDS WELCOME WORKSPACE THAT CAN BE EXTENDED OR SHORTENED AS NEEDED.

Steal This Idea

Order a large chalkboard from a school supply store and hang it on an open wall. It's a perfect spot for grocery lists, important reminders, or enthusiastic greetings!

RIGHT: Wood and metal work together in this kitchen outfitted for a passionate cook. Framed by rustic wooden beams, the professional range has extra burners for multiple pots on the go at once; a collection of gleaming copper pots sits at the ready. The wooden island has an ample worktop and plenty of storage space.

ABOVE: Stripped of its furnishings, this simple square room would look like any newly constructed space. The transformation was effected with beaded-board cabinets, a large hutch, and a long, open plate rack—all of which add character to this otherwise plain space. A white table with a vintage enamel top works as an island. On wheels, it can also be moved if necessary to provide extra seating wherever needed.

A DISTRESSED WOODEN CABINET ADDS TEXTURE TO A CORNER.

L E F T : Who doesn't feel nostalgic for the gentle slam of a screen door? Imagine bringing that sentimental soundtrack into your everyday life. A brand-new screen door, made to look old, shelters the pantry and provides a touch of summer year 'round.

A B O V E : Delft blue sets the tone in this nook and perfectly plays up a collection of blue-and-white vintage plates. The colors are repeated in the checkered cushion. Clean white trim adds a modern feel, while the painted base of the table offers an unexpected and welcome touch of green.

A B O V E : A freestanding cupboard is hung on an exposed
stone wall. The piece is attractive on its own; used to display
a collection of antique ironware, it's irresistible.

R I G H T : A restored refrigerator, farmhouse sink, and
aged furniture create an old farmhouse feel; period-style
details, including light fixtures, sink hardware, and an old
school desk, finish the look.

LEFT: This new kitchen takes its inspiration from Shaker simplicity. Raising cabinets off the floor will make the pieces look more like furniture than built-ins. A few Shaker collectibles, a red bench, and an old pitchfork reinforce the kitchen's theme.

USE OPEN WIRE BASKETS TO STORE AND DISPLAY COLORFUL FRUIT OR LINENS.

Faucet Facts

- Don't scrimp on a faucet. Remember that a kitchen faucet is something you handle every day.
- If you have two side-by-side sinks, consider a faucet that swivels in either direction.

- If counter space is tight, you can mount a faucet directly onto the wall.
- Consider your clean-up needs. A gooseneck faucet allows you to fit tall pots and pans underneath.

A B O V E : A large stainless-steel sink is flanked by a distressed file cabinet and trash container, intelligently mixing industrial design with flea-market chic. Colorful pottery softens the stainless shelves.

ABOVE: A shiny yellow farmhouse sink gets stylish support: simple two-by-fours and exposed copper plumbing give a modern twist to this country basic.

Steal This Idea

Wicker baskets offer more flexibility than permanent drawers. You can carry the basket of silverware or napkins directly to the table.

L E F T : Would you believe this kitchen is a brand new addition? Even if you're planning new construction, you can still successfully execute a rustic, country look. This home relies on reclaimed objects for its sense of history. Old cabinetry and windows, vintage appliances, and a pressed-tin ceiling make this room look like it has been welcoming visitors for decades.

A B O V E : Neo-classical elements create a sense of history in this elegant room. A pair of plaster friezes adorns the wall above the sink, adding a sculptural touch. A corner cabinet decorated with elaborate pilasters anchors the dining area. These unique pieces set the tone for the room and mix beautifully with warm Shaker-inspired cabinetry.

RIGHT: This kitchen is another fine example of how to make new construction look authentically old. The floor was constructed from reclaimed brick. Custom cabinetry was designed to resemble free-standing furniture, such as the dresser-style piece to the side of the range. The new cabinetry was painted a pale yellow to lighten the room, but a strip of walnut remains in the center of the doors for an old-world touch.

A LITTLE ASYMMETRY CAN ADD A LOT OF CHARM. HERE, OLD-FASHIONED TURNED LEGS GRACE ONE SIDE OF THE ISLAND, WHILE A CABINET ANCHORS THE OTHER.

Something to Hide

Kitchen design has come a long way since the days of avocado-green refrigerators and microwaves the size of small cars. But as enamored as you may be with your generously proportioned fridge and double-stacked convection ovens, these and other kitchen necessities can overwhelm a space.

Even if you appreciate the beauty in industrial design, there are many ways to beautifully integrate the necessities into your kitchen without sacrificing style.

If you're a purist, you may want to completely conceal your functional items by camouflaging them with old-world finishes. Another approach is to "retrofit" old treasures into new and useful objects. You need not feel limited by the object's original purpose. Plenty of fabulous furnishings and storage pieces began life as something else entirely, and were repurposed by a visionary home decorator. It is precisely this spirit of resourcefulness and reinvention that is a hallmark of a country kitchen.

WOOD FINISHES NEEDN'T "MATCH"—
A VARIETY OF FINISHES IS A MORE
INTERESTING LOOK.

L E F T : Whether you're working with reproductions or originals, the generous proportions of country furniture make it easy to "retrofit" a piece to cleverly conceal an appliance—or two. This lovely red cabinet, built to look like an armoire, hides a dishwasher and microwave.

ATTENTION TO DETAIL IS CRUCIAL IN CREATING ATTRACTIVE FAUX FRONTS: SIMPLE SHAKER-STYLE MOLDING AND KNOBS MAKE THIS CABINETRY STYLISH AS WELL AS FUNCTIONAL.

A B O V E : With the doors closed, it would be impossible to spot the refrigerator drawers and wall oven disguised by this elegant cabinetry. Hinged doors fold back completely, allowing the oven door to extend. Under-counter freezer drawers, complete with icemaker, are hidden behind faux drawer fronts.

GROOVES EMBEDDED IN THE SOAPSTONE COUNTER OFFER AN INTEGRATED DRAIN BOARD FOR THE DEEP FARMHOUSE SINK.

ABOVE: The front of this dishwasher is finished to match the blue-green cabinets. When closed, the appliance practically disappears.

LEFT: A microwave has become an essential piece of any contemporary kitchen. But where to put it? Too often it takes up precious counter space or valuable cabinet storage. This microwave is mounted in an unused but convenient spot and encased with dark wood to blend in with the rest of the cabinetry.

ABOVE: This imposing farmhouse double sink is softened by a pleated curtain that runs its full length. Offering easy access to while fully disguising everything stored below, it is a stylish option.

A B O V E : Surrounded by blue custom cabinetry, these simple stainless-steel appliances fit in comfortably and do not detract from the room's strong, rustic feel.

A B O V E : If you don't want the insides of your cabinets on constant display, consider frosted glass fronts instead of traditional transparent glass. Frosted glass provides more texture and depth than an opaque front.

LINE GLASS WINDOW PANES WITH ANTIQUE LACE FOR A DELICATE TOUCH OR TO CONCEAL LESS-THAN-PERFECT OBJECTS INSIDE.

R I G H T : A pretty vintage cloth fastened under the sink with clothes pins works perfectly in this "shabby-chic" room. The cloth conceals while simultaneously providing easy access to kitchen supplies.

Lighten Up

Light is a critical factor in every room in a house, but particularly so in the kitchen. It's never too soon to think about the nature of the various light sources in your kitchen and the quality of light that you would like the room to have—during daytime and at night.

Whether you prefer a soft, glowing ambience or strong, bright illumination, you'll need a combination of overall and task lighting for a kitchen that is both practical and pleasant to be in.

Window design, skylights, recessed lighting, pendant placement—all of these sources of light must be decided very early on in the design process. Make sure you're considering a well-balanced mix of lighting: natural light from the outdoors, ambient light to illuminate the entire room, and task lighting for food prep and clean-up. Then choose the right pieces to make your lighting an appealing and essential part of the design. And remember that the right materials and finishes on walls, floors, and countertops can help emphasize all the light sources in the room.

NO BARE CORDS HERE: HANGING FIXTURES GET ADDED APPEAL FROM INDUSTRIAL CHAINS.

L E F T : Don't be afraid to mix and match light fixtures. These fixtures, although different colors, are complementary shapes and recall the same era. The black line around the white pendant connects it nicely to the other two fixtures.

RIGHT: Because all the windows in this room are clustered at one end, the pale wood floor and island effectively extend a sense of light through to the rest of the room. A shiny, white subway-tile backsplash and stainless countertops also reflect the room's natural light.

A COMBINATION OF IN-CEILING LIGHTS (FOR OVERALL BRIGHTNESS) AND HANGING FIXTURES (FOR WORKSPACE ILLUMINATION) IS IDEAL.

ABOVE: Consider lighting the interior of your cabinets as you would an art display case. Interior cabinet lights can add a bright focal point to your kitchen. If you don't want the contents of your cabinets in the spotlight, use frosted glass.

A SMALL STRIP OF MOLDING
HIDES THE FIXTURES.

LEFT: Think about where the most work will take place in your kitchen and then make sure you've installed enough lighting to properly illuminate all those spaces. It's easy to hide small fluorescent lights under the cabinets. Unlike a lot of kitchen lighting, this simple addition can be done even after the cabinets are installed.

LEFT: When privacy is not an issue, maximize natural light by eschewing kitchen curtains. Here, a row of three casement-style windows lets in light and air, with a small café rod on the center window offering a convenient spot for tea towels.

ABOVE: Although it's counterintuitive to place shelving over a window, sometimes it makes sense. In this instance, the window provides an elegant backdrop to a white pottery collection. The delicate white shelf and the iron supports don't interfere with the openness of the window. And because the shelf doesn't block the sight line, it doesn't impede the view. Pulley-style hanging lights over the island further illuminate the room.

L E F T : Window treatments are a quick and easy way to add a decorative touch to a room. To preserve the greatest amount of light, pick a sheer fabric that will let the sun shine through during the day.

Lighting Tips

- Cooktop hood ventilation systems can often be fitted with a light, providing illumination for this important work area.
- Halogen lighting provides dramatic impact and the bulbs last longer, but they also throw off heat—so you won't want to place them where people will be sitting, working, or congregating.
- When choosing shades or covers for pendant lights, make sure the material can be easily cleaned. A fabric shade might look prettier than glass, but is much more difficult to clean.

ABOVE: A dining alcove in this kitchen benefits from a wealth of natural light courtesy of wrap-around windows and a back door that opens to the yard. Sheer curtains can be used for privacy while allowing in light; at night, a simple chandelier casts a soft glow, creating a romantic ambience. Note how the dark cabinetry serves to ground the room.

ABOVE: Natural and artificial light floods this kitchen in all the right places. The sink is positioned under two roomy windows, illuminating a key workspace. A skylight adds crucial natural light to this relatively low-ceilinged room. The white beaded-board backsplash is higher than usual, extending several feet up from the countertop and enhancing the room's airy feel. Pendant lights add important spot lighting to the center island.

SHEER BLINDS ARE SIMPLE
AND UNOBTRUSIVE, ALLOWING
LIGHT IN WHILE PRESERVING
PRIVACY.

Photography Credits

Page 1: Keith Scott Morton
Page 2: William P. Steele
Page 3: Keith Scott Morton
Page 5 top: Natasha Milne
Page 5 middle: Steven Randazzo
Page 5 bottom: Keith Scott Morton
Page 6: Keith Scott Morton
Page 9: William P. Steele
Page 10: Keith Scott Morton
Page 13: Phillip Clayton-Thompson
Page 14: Keith Scott Morton
Page 16: Keith Scott Morton
Page 17: Michael Luppino
Page 18: Jeff McNamara
Page 19: Jeff McNamara
Page 20: Keith Scott Morton
Page 21: Peter Margonelli
Page 22: Keith Scott Morton
Page 23: Michael Luppino
Page 25: William P. Steele
Page 26 top: Ray Kachatorian
Page 26 bottom: Ray Kachatorian
Page 27: Ray Kachatorian
Page 28: Natasha Milne
Page 30: Keith Scott Morton
Page 33: Keith Scott Morton
Page 34: Keith Scott Morton
Page 35: Keith Scott Morton
Page 36: Michael Luppino
Page 37: Keith Scott Morton
Page 39: Gridley & Graves
Page 40: Keith Scott Morton
Page 43: William P. Steele
Page 44: Keith Scott Morton
Page 45: Jessie Walker
Page 47: Keith Scott Morton
Page 48: Keith Scott Morton
Page 49: William P. Steele

Page 50: Keith Scott Morton
Page 51: Keith Scott Morton
Page 52: James Merrell
Page 55: Grey Crawford
Page 56: Jeremy Samuelson
Page 57: Jonn Coolidge
Page 58: Tim Street-Porter
Page 61: Mark Lohman
Page 62: Steven Randazzo
Page 64: Keith Scott Morton
Page 66: Steven Randazzo
Page 67: Keith Scott Morton
Page 68: William P. Steele
Page 69: William P. Steele
Page 71: Jeff McNamara
Page 72: Gridley & Graves
Page 74: Michael Luppino
Page 75: Keith Scott Morton
Page 76: Robin Stubbert
Page 77: Keith Scott Morton
Page 78: Keith Scott Morton
Page 80: William P. Steele
Page 81: John Gruen
Page 82: Keith Scott Morton
Page 84: Michael Luppino
Page 85: Mark Lohman
Page 86: John Bessler
Page 87: Jessie Walker
Page 88: Keith Scott Morton
Page 89: Keith Scott Morton
Page 90: Grey Crawford
Page 93: Charles Maraia
Page 94: Keith Scott Morton
Page 95: Keith Scott Morton
Page 96: William P. Steele
Page 97: Keith Scott Morton
Page 98: Robin Stubbert
Page 101: Keith Scott Morton

Page 102: Michael Luppino
Page 103: Keith Scott Morton
Page 104: Keith Scott Morton
Page 105: Keith Scott Morton
Page 106: Keith Scott Morton
Page 108 top: Keith Scott Morton
Page 108 bottom: Robin Stubbert
Page 109: Keith Scott Morton
Page 110: William P. Steele
Page 111: Michael Luppino
Page 112: Steven Randazzo
Page 113: Michael Luppino
Page 114: Keith Scott Morton
Page 116: Keith Scott Morton
Page 117: Michael Luppino
Page 118: Steven Randazzo
Page 119: Steven Randazzo
Page 121: Gridley & Graves
Page 122: Keith Scott Morton
Page 124 left: Jessie Walker
Page 124 right: Jessie Walker
Page 125: Keith Scott Morton
Page 126: Robin Stubbert
Page 127: Keith Scott Morton
Page 128 right: Keith Scott Morton
Page 128 left: Jeff McNamara
Page 129: Michael Luppino
Page 130: Keith Scott Morton
Page 133: William P. Steele
Page 134: William P. Steele
Page 135: Keith Scott Morton
Page 136: Rob Melnychuk
Page 137: Keith Scott Morton
Page 138: Michael Luppino
Page 139: Keith Scott Morton
Page 140: Keith Scott Morton

Index

Note: Page numbers in *italics* refer to illustrations

Index Continued